Disney Songs for Xylophone

Arranged by Will Rapp

ISBN 978-1-5400-8216-9

Visit Hal Leonard Online at
www.halleonard.com

Contact us:
Hal Leonard
7777 West Bluemound Road
Milwaukee, WI 53213
Email: info@halleonard.com

In Europe, contact:
Hal Leonard Europe Limited
42 Wigmore Street
Marylebone, London, W1U 2RN
Email: info@halleonardeurope.com

In Australia, contact:
Hal Leonard Australia Pty. Ltd.
4 Lentara Court
Cheltenham, Victoria, 3192 Australia
Email: info@halleonard.com.au

BE OUR GUEST

from BEAUTY AND THE BEAST

XYLOPHONE

Music by ALAN MENKEN
Lyrics by HOWARD ASHMAN

BEAUTY AND THE BEAST

from BEAUTY AND THE BEAST

XYLOPHONE

Music by ALAN MENKEN
Lyrics by HOWARD ASHMAN

BIBBIDI-BOBBIDI-BOO

(The Magic Song)

from CINDERELLA

XYLOPHONE

Words by JERRY LIVINGSTON
Music by MACK DAVID and AL HOFFMAN

CRUELLA DE VIL

from 101 DALMATIANS

XYLOPHONE

Words and Music by
MEL LEVEN

A DREAM IS A WISH YOUR HEART MAKES

from CINDERELLA

XYLOPHONE

Music by MACK DAVID and AL HOFFMAN
Lyrics by JERRY LIVINGSTON

DO YOU WANT TO BUILD A SNOWMAN?

from FROZEN

XYLOPHONE

Music and Lyrics by KRISTEN ANDERSON-LOPEZ
and ROBERT LOPEZ

Wood Blocks
W. Blk.
Slower
mp
mf
f
p

GIVE A LITTLE WHISTLE

from PINOCCHIO

XYLOPHONE

Words by NED WASHINGTON
Music by LEIGH HARLINE

8va
8va
(8va)
8va
8va
8va
8va

GOD HELP THE OUTCASTS

from THE HUNCHBACK OF NOTRE DAME

XYLOPHONE

Music by ALAN MENKEN
Lyrics by STEPHEN SCHWARTZ

HE'S A TRAMP

from LADY AND THE TRAMP

XYLOPHONE

Words and Music by PEGGY LEE
and SONNY BURKE

I JUST CAN'T WAIT TO BE KING

from THE LION KING

XYLOPHONE

Music by ELTON JOHN
Lyrics by TIM RICE

mp
mf
f

I SEE THE LIGHT

from TANGLED

XYLOPHONE

Music by ALAN MENKEN
Lyrics by GLENN SLATER

f
f
mp

KISS THE GIRL

from THE LITTLE MERMAID

XYLOPHONE

Music by ALAN MENKEN
Lyrics by HOWARD ASHMAN

MICKEY MOUSE MARCH

from THE MICKEY MOUSE CLUB

XYLOPHONE

Words and Music by
JIMMIE DODD

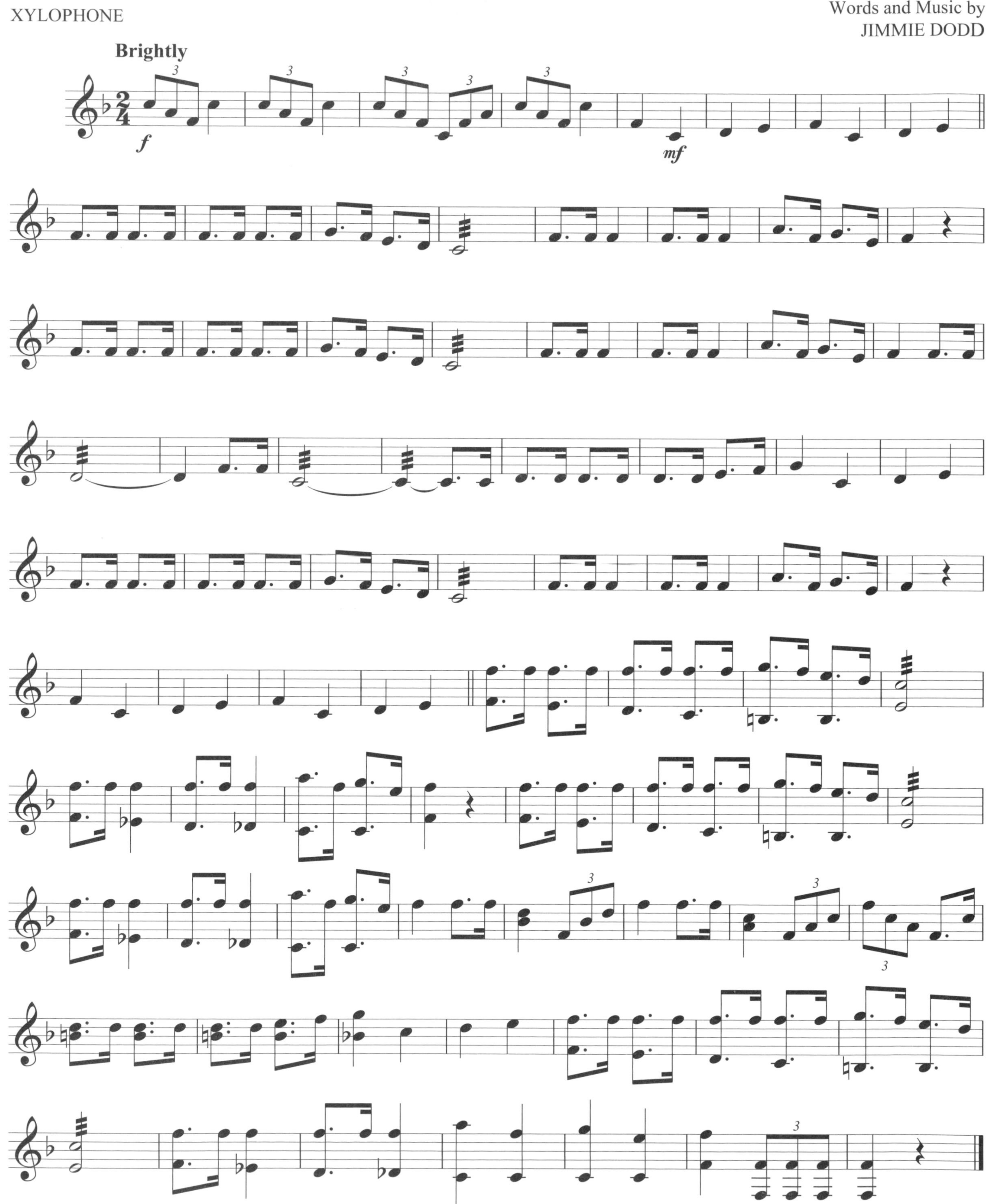

NEVER TOO LATE

from THE LION KING (2019)

XYLOPHONE

Music by ELTON JOHN
Lyrics by TIM RICE

mp
mf
f
mf

f
mf

A SPOONFUL OF SUGAR

from MARY POPPINS

XYLOPHONE

Words and Music by RICHARD M. SHERMAN
and ROBERT B. SHERMAN

WHEN SHE LOVED ME

from TOY STORY 2

XYLOPHONE

Music and Lyrics by
RANDY NEWMAN

THAT'S HOW YOU KNOW

from ENCHANTED

XYLOPHONE

Music by ALAN MENKEN
Lyrics by STEPHEN SCHWARTZ

mf

WHEN YOU WISH UPON A STAR

from PINOCCHIO

XYLOPHONE

Words by NED WASHINGTON
Music by LEIGH HARLINE

A WHOLE NEW WORLD
(Aladdin's Theme)
from ALADDIN

XYLOPHONE

Music by ALAN MENKEN
Lyrics by TIM RICE

WHISTLE WHILE YOU WORK

from SNOW WHITE AND THE SEVEN DWARFS

XYLOPHONE

Words by LARRY MOREY
Music by FRANK CHURCHILL

f
mp
mf

WINNIE THE POOH

from THE MANY ADVENTURES OF WINNIE THE POOH

XYLOPHONE

Words and Music by RICHARD M. SHERMAN
and ROBERT B. SHERMAN

Based on the "Winnie the Pooh" works, by A. A. Milne and E. H. Shepard

YO HO

(A Pirate's Life For Me)

from Disney Parks' Pirates of the Caribbean attraction

XYLOPHONE

Words by XAVIER ATENCIO
Music by GEORGE BRUNS

YOU'RE WELCOME

from MOANA

XYLOPHONE

Music and Lyrics by
LIN-MANUEL MIRANDA

3
3

YOU'VE GOT A FRIEND IN ME

from TOY STORY

XYLOPHONE

Music and Lyrics by
RANDY NEWMAN

f
mf
rit.
a tempo
mp

YOU'LL BE IN MY HEART
(Pop Version)
from TARZAN™

XYLOPHONE

Words and Music by
PHIL COLLINS

mf
f